SHAWNEE PEAK
AT PLEASANT MOUNTAIN
Maine's oldest continuously operated ski area

By David Irons
Foreword by Marty Basch

Contents

Pleasant Mountain, In the Beginning
Maine's First Ski Patrol
Memories from Walter Soule
The Downeast Ski Club
Big Improvements in the Fifties
The Jenni Era
The Seventies and Eight Owners
Pleasant Mountain Freestyle
Opening the 1978 Season
New Owners After the No Snow Winter
The Shawnee Group
Haggett Memorial Fund
Chet Homer Becomes the Owner
The Ice Storm
The Modern Ski School
The Modern Ski Patrol
The Moonlight Charity Challenge
The Adaptive Skiing Program
Mountain Dew
A Summer Day
Ed Rock's Retirement
Shawnee Peak at 80
Skiers From Away
The Future
Recognition
Shawnee Peak Skiers in the Maine Ski Hall of Fame

Cover photos
The front cover shows Shawnee Peak as it appears today at night.
The inset is from a brochure furnished by the Bridgton Historical Society, showing the trail map as it appeared between the first T-bar installation in 1951 and the first chair lift in 1954.
Back cover
This Bruce Cole photo shows the Pines Slope double chair with
Mount Washington in the back ground.

Dedication

This book is dedicated to all of those early skiers who were not content to simply climb the hill to ski down. Instead they put up the rope tows that got it all started and went on to add T-bars and chair lifts. And to those who in the years since have taken the risks to make ski areas grow to serve the skiers with even better lifts and conditions. None love our sport more and they deserve the thanks of all skiers.

Foreword
By Marty Basch

For me, Shawnee Peak has always been a pleasant mountain. It rises proudly above a patchwork of farms and forests in western Maine. To see the cascading trails from U.S. Route 302 with frozen Moose Pond in the forefront is to know that cruising those grin-inducing trails is imminent. Even before making those glorious first turns down the Bridgton peak any stress melts away when you're whisked up to summit with those views across two states of frozen lakes and the frosted Presidential Range in neighboring New Hampshire. Toddlers, tweens, teens and skiers of all ages can find happiness on its slopes.

Shawnee is an anchor of Maine skiing history. The state's first t-bar and first chairlift were installed at Shawnee. It's seen a number of owners since its infancy and over the years it's moved ahead at its own Yankee-style pace.

That's the beauty of the place. It's a place to kick back and unwind on trails like the snaking Lower Kancamagus, straight Lower Appalachian, the great combination of Jack Spratt, The Horn, the Headwall and East Slope, and Sunset Boulevard. Find those pockets of pow off the summit, or those surprising hidden trails like Fat and Happy and Beeline. Mellow out on Happiness Is and Pine Slope. Hit the park on The Main.

Of course, there have been pioneers at the mountain like the first and second general managers, Nelson Turner and Jack Spratt along with another founder, Russ Haggett, who returned from service in World War II to serve as general manager from 1946 to 1978. General manager Ed Rock, a Shawnee stalwart and all-around-nice-guy for decades, recently retired and a weekend doesn't go by when pass holders, day trippers and others could easily bump into owner Chet Homer—Dartmouth grad, former AHL Portland Pirates co-owner and onetime-exec-vice president and director of Tom's of Maine —in the base lodge. Homer's been a good steward of Shawnee since buying it in 1994. He's invested millions.

I was brought back to those Shawnee characters and others on a frigid January Saturday night in 2013 in the base lodge's Blizzard's Pub. It was the ski area's 75th anniversary and I had been asked to say a few words about the mountain.

So had Dave Irons.

I've known Dave since, well, back during the days when I had hair. Dave still has his, far too much I think, and never skis with a hat on. A noted ski historian, Maine Ski Hall of Fame member, ski patroller, writer and broadcaster, we've known each other for decades in our capacities as wordsmiths.

Dave, a Westbrook skier, spent his formative days at Shawnee when it was called Pleasant Mountain.

With his gift of loquaciousness, Dave took those in the packed room back to the days when the mountain had more cows than skiers. It was the 1930s and skiers from Portland would venture to Mount Washington with their long wooden skis to challenge themselves on the northeast's highest peak. But soon enough, they wanted someplace closer.

Pleasant Mountain was talked about.

So one day some skiers sought out the owner of the land on the mountain. It was a farmer named Harry Douglas. They asked if they could ski on his land.

They could. But there was one thing they had to do.

"You can ski but you have to put the fences back up for my cows in spring," he said according to Dave.

Today, skiers easily outnumber the cows. There's no high-speed quad. There's more trailside accommodations but nothing too daunting. Heck, there's even a yurt and cabin on the summit to spend the night.

Afternoon school buses are mid-week parking lot staples as young Mainers learn to ski. When the sun goes down the lights go on with plenty of opportunity to make turns and have some adult fun especially if you take part in the spirited Racing with the Moon Series. And those lights. You can readily see the love radiating along U.S. Route 302 from Shawnee with keen eyes seeing l-o-v spelled out by those lights illuminating the trails.

With all the material available to him, Dave's the man to write the book about Shawnee Peak. He's skied its slopes for more than half a century. He's immersed in its history. He's accumulated a wealth of personal information and experience to bring the mountain and its devotees to life in these pages. Sprinkled with vintage photos, trail maps and other Shawnee treats, he's captured the essence of the laid-back ski area that continues to enhance western Maine's skiing lifestyle embraced by so many for generations and years to come.

Introduction

Pleasant Mountain ~ Shawnee Peak

Putting together any history is a challenge as I learned when writing a book on a ski area 50 years old. Add 30 years to that and the challenge grows. At fifty years it's difficult to find more than a handful who actually built the ski area, but at 80 years, there is no one left who was actually part of the original building. Fortunately, I had the task in 1978 of writing a feature article on the occasion of the 40th anniversary of Pleasant Mountain and I was able to go back to that piece for some information. I also had the benefit of nearly forty years of writing about skiing in Maine and my files included press kits from Pleasant Mountain and Shawnee Peak, along with articles I had written for annual newspaper ski supplements. Digging through those pieces I was able to pinpoint which improvements happened year by year.

It was also important to look back on my own experience which dates back to skiing Pleasant Mountain in the fifties when we were quite content to have a T-bar and a Chair lift to get us up the mountain. Over the years I was able to watch the growth of Maine's oldest continuously operated commercial ski area.

Certainly, I could have written a general history of Shawnee Peak and Pleasant Mountain from my own memory and records, but I knew there was more. Bruce Chalmers directed me to Al Ordway who filled me in on how his parents had run the ski school. A delightful afternoon with Hans and Barbara Jenni helped me understand the sixties and a phone call to Judy Genesio helped to appreciate how difficult it must have been for her father, Russ Haggett to live at and operate the fledgling ski area after the war.

Ted Logan filled me in on the seventies when he and seven others owned the ski area while operating their own businesses in the Portland area, where a large portion of loyal skiers still live and work. Conversations over the years with Tom Bennett, Don Wyman and Frank Emery gave me an insight into the Downeast Ski Club along with friendships with a number of members. My own experience as a ski patrolman had brought me in contact with Jimmy Jones and other members of the Pleasant Mountain patrol so I could easily put that story together.

Ned Allen and Lega Medcalf at the Bridgton Historical Society provided me with important articles from the Bridgton News and some of the images of early brochures that are found in these pages.

Interviews in person and by phone with past and current skiers gave me an understanding of how these skiers viewed Shawnee Peak at Pleasant Mountain. Most started skiing there in the fifties and sixties and have watched the changes and growth over the years. My own experience skiing there several times a season for the past 30 years gave me an intimate knowledge of the mountain, its runs and the friendly lifties.
Watching my grandchildren learn to ski at Shawnee Peak added to the experience.

All of these helped me put this story together, but two people helped the most, Ed Rock and Chet Homer. I have known Ed since he arrived 34 years ago and he has always been accommodating and up front with answers to my questions. He filled in a lot of blanks. While I had met Chet when he first acquired the ski area, I had never really had an extended talk with him until five years ago when I started this project. I hope I have adequately portrayed his passion for the sport and the ski area he owns but considers himself a steward, whose responsibility is to keep the operation up to date, provide a great ski experience for today's skiers while preserving it for the next generation.

I'm sure that this book will stir memories among other regular skiers at Shawnee Peak. I welcome their input because I know there is more to this story and I will be happy to add to what I have written for some future volume. For now, this is the basic story of Pleasant Mountain, those who built the ski area in the beginning and who made it grow through the years. And the more recent story of Shawnee Peak as we celebrate 80 years of skiing at this venerable ski area.

Finally, there is one individual I want to recognize. Digging up the stories, locating trail maps and pictures make up only part of the project. Once the material is in hand and the text written a book must be created. Proper formatting and placement of images is critical to making any book readable. For this I turned to Bo Bigelow who does just about everything for Ski Maine. I don't know how many hours Bo invested in this project, but I do know that without his considerable computer skills you would not have this attractive publication in your hands.

PLEASANT MOUNTAIN, IN THE BEGINNING

In the thirties skiers needed a true devotion to the sport. Those who skied accepted the mountains as they were, with few lifts or groomed trails, and no comfortable base lodges in which to change. Of course, there was no real need to change as they drove to the slopes wearing their ankle high leather boots. Once on the hill they could climb with climbing skins, by traversing back and forth, sidestepping or herringboning up. They could ski down through the unpacked snow or pack the runs by sidestepping up.

Turning the heavy wood skis was a challenge, with bindings that combined a toe iron with either leather straps or metal spring cables. Skis were measured by how high the skier could reach with most skis ranging from 6' 6" to 7' 6". Yet, with these awkward instruments, skiers would travel from Portland, all the way to Mount Washington to ski in Tuckerman Ravine and down the Sherburne Ski Trail back to the highway in Pinkham Notch.

As these skiers drove along Rte 302, they passed by Pleasant Mountain, towering above Moose Pond, and thinking it would be nice to have a ski hill closer to home investigated skiing the open slopes on the lower mountain. Those lower slopes were actually pastures where cattle belonging to Harry Douglas grazed in the summer months. When approached by the skiers, Douglas was happy to accommodate their desires on the condition that the fences be replaced before it was time for the cattle to return in the spring. Before long the Portland skiers were joined by local skiers from the Bridgton area led by

This is probably the earliest pin for Pleasant Mountain sometime in the forties provided by the late Al Ordway.

Early Mountain Photo: This was the view of the ski area in the early years. Note the single run from the top which had to be climbed to ski before the chair lift in 1954.

Russ Haggett and students from Bridgton Academy.

Not satisfied with skiing just those lower pastures, they were soon cutting trails further up the mountain under the direction of Harry Sampson, then headmaster of Bridgton Academy. In 1936, they convinced the C.C.C. (The Civilian Conservation Corps formed under Roosevelt to put men to work during the depression) to cut a trail from the top of the mountain. Not realizing that the skiers were capable of making turns on a downhill pitch, the C.C.C.workers used the logs they cut to create banked turns of 25-30 degrees. The new run was named the Wayshego trail and Pleasant Mountain had skiing from the ledges at the summit to the Mountain Road more than 1000 feet below.

Looking for more, the Bridgton Chamber of Commerce got involved in 1937 leasing the property with annual renewals and an option to buy within four years. On the newly leased land a 16 by 32 foot shelter was built and a rope tow installed. The official opening took place January 23, 1938 and over 500 were on hand to celebrate winter skiing off an 1100 foot rope tow. The party also included tobogganing, ski jumping, ice skating and hot lunches served out of the shelter.

In the fifties skiers could buy skiing by the run. The book containing 20 coupons, cost $5.00. Riding the chair cost 2 tickets and the T-Bar 1 ticket. The faster East T-bar took one and half tickets. It worked for skiers who could not get in enough runs to use up the book in a single day. Those of us who skied at faster speeds bought an all day pass for $4.00 and unless lift lines were very long we always exceeded the ten Chair rides or 20 T-bar rides.

Wes Marco taught skiing on the slopes before the lift went up and taught that first season. In his words, "In those days most skiers could only turn one way and I could turn both ways so they made me ski instructor." Nelson Turner was the first area manager, followed by Jack Spratt in 1939. A small group formed the Pleasant Mountain Ski Club, Ray Riley, Russ Haggett, Luke Evans, Sid Russell, Jack Spratt and Wes Marco.

The Bridgton News reported November 8. 1940 that at a special meeting at the Town House, the town voted to purchase the property owned by Harry L. Douglas for $800.

According to the late Frank Emery, Haggett, Marco, Riley and Evans joined forces to form the Pleasant Mountain Corporation and purchase the land from the town and the Evans family. By 1945 there were three rope tows, one above the other in the center of the main slope and the third to the right of the main slope, which also served a jump. Marco moved to Bridgton from his home in Bath and managed the area that season. Haggett and

Evans served with the Seabees, the construction division of the Navy in the Pacific during the war returning in 1946.

At that time Haggett took over as General Manager and in 1947 when Marco was recalled to the shipyard at Bath Ironworks he sold his share in the mountain to Haggett. Under Haggett a string of improvements were started that would continue for three decades of his management. That first year he oversaw the cutting of trees for glade skiing to the west of the main slope and enlarging the base lodge. Even with just rope tows, the ski area grew in popularity becoming the favorite place for Portland skiers to pursue their sport.

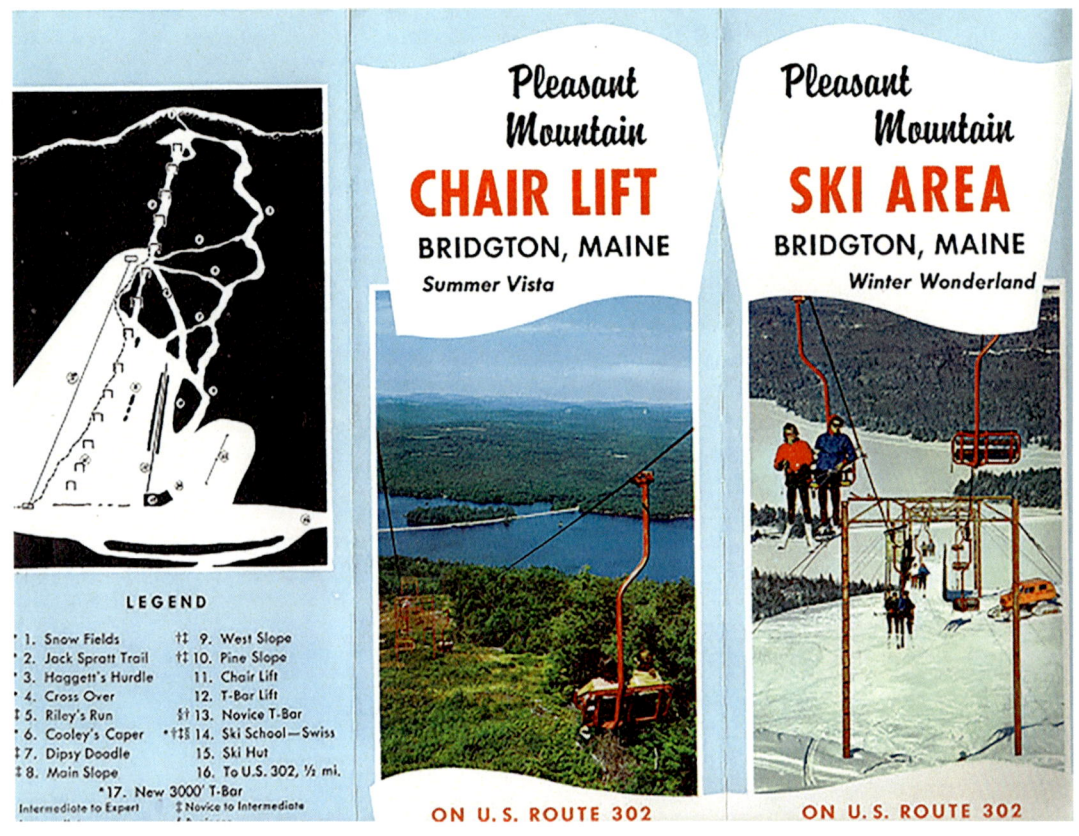

This brochure is from the mid to late sixties.

In 1946, the base lodge was nothing more than a 16 X 32 foot ski hut and for three years it was also home for the young Haggett family, wife Geneva and daughter Judy. The following written by Judy Genesio appeared first in the Bridgton News and later in Connections, a publication of the Bridgton Historical Society.

"Sixty years ago there was an outhouse standing alone in a wooded area at the foot of Pleasant Mountain. I'm sure there are skiers around who remember the "four holer". But I know that I am the only one left who called it my bathroom. Stationed as it was on the opposite side of the parking lot behind the "ski hut", it could be formidable undertaking for a little girl waiting in line with the winter ski crowd.

3

This patch represents the Pleasant Mountain Ski Club, about 1957.

Some who remember the original ski hut may not have seen the private room adjacent to the kitchen that was ours alone, but most, I think, did not. The "hut" consisted of a large room divided into a kitchen and sitting area that served double duty as the family living area in the summer and the skiers' lounging area in the winter. The private room I shared with my parents was large enough for a double bed separated from my cot by sheeting. There was no running water and a wood stove in the front room provided heat.

My memories of the years between four and seven do not include the hardships my parents must have endured. I enjoyed a huge front yard full of happy friendly people in the winter and unlimited opportunities to explore when my city cousins visited during the summer months. We had a large garden that probably supplied most of our vegetables. Milk and eggs came from the Evans farm out on Route 302, and my father hunted each fall, fished year round and often traded for meat. (Genesio's mom, Geneva created the meals for the skiers who dined with the family.)

In 1949, we left the hut to the skiers and moved into town. Only later did I connect that move to the birth of my sister, Janet. Even my enterprising, frontier parents apparently couldn't figure out how to manage two kids in the ski hut. Being a "townie" was fun: my world now included friends that weren't imaginary or four–legged. Five years later my sister Jackie was born and our house-hopping days ended when we settled in West Bridgton to be closer to my father's beloved Pleasant Mountain.

The remainder of my school years, the routine of "the mountain" governed the lives of the Haggett household. During the summer months, talk was about maintenance and growth. The winter months were a bit tenser. Without snowmaking equipment, weather reports were critical. Each day began with phoned in ski reports and ended with hours of trail grooming. Looking back as an adult I understand how hard my parents worked and how little we experienced of the material world, but looking up at the mountain with multiple lifts. all in lights and a robust business in full swing, I know that my father, a farm boy from West Bridgton, was one of the fortunate few who realized his childhood dream."

In those times, everyone bought their tickets by the day, but one young Bridgton student had another idea in 1952. As Bruce Chalmers tells the story, he didn't want to have to ask his father for a dollar whenever he wanted to ski, "So I asked Mr. Haggett about a season pass and he sold me the first one ever for $15.00."

After the war Newell Ordway and his wife Helen ran the ski school. As the story goes, Newell had taught Wes Marco to ski before the lifts in exchange for Marco an accomplished golfer teaching Ordway that sport. Their son Al Ordway, remembered Haggett's father, Russ Sr. moving about the base area, clad in a great overcoat, selling lift tickets while chewing on a cigar.

Naturally some of those skiers took a keen interest in the area and in 1947, Ray Erickson, an engineer from Cape Elizabeth purchased the property from the three remaining shareholders, Haggett, Evans and Riley. Joining in the purchase were Al Cooley from Falmouth and Emil Morin from Danville and plans for improvements were developed.

It was in 1948 that a group was formed that would provide some of the area's strongest supporters. The Downeast Ski Club was an outgrowth of the Portland YMCA's social group known as the Gay 20s Club. Led by Tom Bennett, the group organized bus trips to Peasant Mountain.

MAINE'S FIRST SKI PATROL

Maine's first ski patrol grew out of a meeting at Portland High School in 1936 where Domie Lowell, then Eastern Division Director of the fledgling National Ski Patrol explained how to create a patrol. One of the attendees, James Jones took the directions and became the leader of the first ski patrol in Maine, a municipal patrol called the Forest City Ski Patrol. The intent was to offer their services to any ski area that could use them, but as the only real ski area in the state at the time, Pleasant Mountain was where they patrolled.

In those days the only requirement was completing the Red Cross Standard and Advanced First Aid courses and Jones earned his instructor rating, which led to his training many future patrollers, including one Robert "Stub" Taylor who became the first patrolman at Sugarloaf and directed that patrol for more than 40 years.

In 1938 Jones became patrol leader at Pleasant Mountain, a position he held until 1972. Under his direction the Pleasant Mountain patrol was a leader in all thing ski patrol in Maine. In those early years training was informal and Jones and his team played a key role in developing standards and training in

Jimmy Jones, the first ski patrol director in Maine overseeing some ski patrol practice.

procedures and toboggan handling and other necessary patrol skills. When various levels were introduced with the goal of most patrollers to earn the Senior designation, Jim Jones became the first head of ski and toboggan testing in Maine. Under his leadership, Pleasant Mountain was a headquarters for ski patrolling in Maine.

Pleasant Mountain ski patrollers at work.

A group of Pleasant Mountain ski patrollers in the traditional rust colored parks of the early days of the National Ski Patrol.

MEMORIES FROM WALTER SOULE

We used to drive from Portland to ski on Mount Washington and we would look up and see this big pasture on a hillside in Bridgton. We finally found out who owned it and he told us we could take down some barbed wire fences if we put them back in the spring.

There was a group from Portland, two or three car loads, that would park out on the main road and ski in. We had been there for a few Sundays when Russ Haggett and some of the boys from Bridgton skied in to see what was going on. That was the start of the Pleasant Mountain Ski Club. The group of us all became charter members.

This photo was featured on the cover of the AAA magazine December, 1968. Note the long thong bindings, which disappeared about that time with the advances in binding technology.

We got the C.C.C. (Civilian Conservation Corps) to come in and build us a rope tow and clear some of the slopes. They didn't realize we could make a turn on a downhill slopes, so they built a trail from the top of the mountain with corduroy turns for us. They dug holes in the trail and used the logs from the slopes to make a big banked turn of 25-30 degrees. There were times when guys would go right over the edge and land in the trees. I

don't remember anyone getting seriously hurt.
(This was excerpted from The Pleasant Times a collection of stories and insights gathered by Glenn Parkinson in 1992)

THE DOWNEAST SKI CLUB

This Downeast Ski Club Lodge sits just beyond the east end of the main parking lot.

In 1948 Tom Bennett was part of a group associated with the Portland YMCA looking for outdoor activity. Under the Y's Gay 20's Club, this group provided opportunities for returning GI's to dance and attend other social activities, but they were more interested in outdoor recreation. According to Bennett this led to organized hikes in the fall and bus trips to Pleasant Mountain to ski. This offshoot from the Y formed the Downeast Ski Club and soon skiing at Pleasant Mountain was a regular part of the club.

Every Sunday morning they had a bus pick up the group to ski for the day and return to Portland at night. Some within the group stayed at a camp on the Mountain Road and decided it would be great for the club to have a place of their own. They approached Russ Haggett and he sold them an acre of land adjacent to the ski area for $50. Bennett pointed out that at that time it wasn't so adjacent with nearly 500 yards separating the property from the base lodge. Today the entire space between is occupied by the parking lot. They cleared a cross country trail to the base lodge and cut trails from the mountain so they could ski back to the lodge.

Bennett credits Ray Riley, one of the Mountain's owners, as taking an interest in the club and encouraging them to build the lodge much larger than the 20 X 30 structure they envisioned. With only 88 members paying just $2 in dues there was little money in the till to finance such a project so they set out to raise the funds with raffles, Scotch auctions and finally ski movies when they appeared on the scene. The first and most important fund raiser was simple, but in those days it was asking a lot. Each member was asked to pledge $10 at a time when $30-40 was a week's pay. Tom said, "It wasn't easy but all 88 members contributed."

They built the lodge and it continues today to be the heart of a group that has boosted Pleasant Mountain more than 60 of its 80 year history.

An indication of how the club members involvement with the mountain is more than just skiing is an annual Chili dinner at the club house where the staff at the mountain is invited as guests. Various club members cook their own versions of chili and the workers at the mountain, be they lifties, snowmakers ski patrol, cafeteria workers or any job at the area, judge the results of the different recipes.

Over the years numerous club members have been ski instructors and patrollers. They also serve to spread the word around southern Maine about the attributes of skiing at Shawnee Peak, a volunteer marketing team.

BIG IMPROVEMENTS IN THE FIFTIES

The new owners, Erickson, Cooley and Morin, wasted no time in putting their plans

SNOW CONDITIONS . . .
- ★ Northeast Exposure accepted as best for maintaining snow.
- ★ Skiing from late December until early April.
- ★ Wonderful Spring Skiing during March and first part of April.

New Improvements to the Ski Slopes

GENERAL FACILITIES . . .
- ★ 4,300 ft. DOUBLE CHAIR LIFT
- ★ 2,000 ft. CONSTAM T-BAR
- ★ 700 ft. T-BAR, NOVICE AREA
- ★ ROPE TOW for Beginners
- ★ SKI HUT, Two-story and balcony
- ★ SNACK BAR
- ★ SKI SHOP
- ★ SKI SCHOOL—Certified

ACCESSIBILITY . . .
Easily Reached by Auto
- ★ From Boston use Maine Turnpike to Portland and Route 302 to Bridgton, Maine.
- ★ From North Conway, N.H., 20 miles east on Route 302.
- ★ Area ¼ mile off Route 302 on a good road.

The Only Chair Lift in Maine
Designed by E. G. Constam
Noted lift engineer of Denver, Colorado

THIS DOUBLE CHAIR LIFT
is equipped with modern safety devices for your protection.

A 12-min. ride takes you 4,300' to the top of Pleasant Mountain, where you pause to enjoy the wonderful scenery . . . then take off for the 1¼-mile run to the Ski Hut, or cut across the Dipsy Doodle to the top of the Main Slope and then to the base station of the Chair Lift.

400 Skiers per hour can enjoy riding our Double Chair Lift

Our 2,000-ft. Constam T-Bar
serves the Main Slope, for expert and intermediate skiers, and the West Slope, where the intermediate and novice can enjoy a ½-mile run to the Ski Hut.

800 rides per hour keep waiting time to a minimum.

Our New Novice T-Bar
is thoroughly enjoyed by the beginners, who almost always graduate to the larger lifts before the season is over.

This was a flyer in the mid fifties promoting Pleasant Mountain with Maine's first and only chair lift.

This was the first T-bar in Maine which ran up between what is now the Pine Slope and the Main. Skiers today can ski a narrow run between those trails where the T-bar once ran. Notice how small the base lodge was in those early years.

Russ Haggett loads Ray Erickson on the first T-bar installed in 1951.

While Russ Haggett ran things on the mountain, his wife Polly kept things running smoothly in the office.

in motion, cutting new trails and in 1951 replacing one of the rope tows with Maine's first T-bar. With Haggett staying on as manager, a new base lodge was built, parking expanded and grooming equipment acquired. In 1954, Pleasant Mountain hit the big time with the state's first chair lift which would carry skiers to the summit and the top of the Jack Spratt trail.

A July 2nd piece in the Portland Press Herald carried the headline, "Maine's Only Chair Lift To Be Placed In Operation"

The article written by Jack Quinn the local correspondent out of South Paris, went on, "In a few days Maine's only chair lift – the third longest in New England – will be in full operation at the Pleasant Mountain development overlooking Moose Pond. Construction of the 4,300 foot lift to the top of the north peak is progressing rapidly."

This weekend will see the wheels turning on the ponderous machinery which drives the 8,600 foot, inch thick steel cable along the 17 towers stretching from the valley station more than 2000 feet above sea level. Then the next ten days operators will devote their time to the experimental work of getting all the kinks out of the newest addition to Maine's scenic attractions."

The piece continued describing the 100 horsepower electric engine and the 125 horsepower gas auxiliary engine, the automatic brakes on the 72 chair lift. Views from the top were cited, 12 lakes including Sebago, the Presidential Range and on clear days Portland Harbor. Details of the construction were spelled out, hauling tons of steel and concrete up the mountain with a small tractor 1000 pounds at a time, erecting the towers, and building the base terminal.

The lengthy story concluded with information on how the ski hut would be opened for the summer and tickets could be purchased to ride the new lift. The final sentence stated, ""Haggett said that the development

officials plan the official opening program in the fall, when Maine is resplendent in its fall foliage".

While the addition of summer business was important the anticipation of skiers was for the coming ski season. More skiers at the top of the mountain meant more ways down were needed and Haggett's Hurdle, still one of the steepest runs on the mountain, was cut to the west. From this run skiers could also take breaks to check spectacular views of Mount Washington and the entire Presidential Range. As the only ski area in the state offering a T-bar and a chair lift, Pleasant Mountain quickly became a very busy place.

To handle the increasing numbers of skiers improvements were needed on and off the mountain. In 1958, the parking area was enlarged and Haggett's widened. The following year, Jack Spratt was widened and in 1960, the west wing was added to the base lodge, providing space for additional rest rooms, an enlarged retail shop and first aid room. Outside the parking area was enlarged again, and five acres of slope cleared and a T-bar erected for novices.

THE JENNI ERA

Pleasant Mountain Ski School patch under Hans Jenni.

By the late fifties, Pleasant Mountain was a busy ski area owned by Ray Erickson, Al Cooley, Ray Riley and Russ Haggett, with Haggett managing the area. Looking to elevate the ski school to the next level, Haggett brought Hans Jenni who had come from Switzerland to teach for Paul Valar at Cannon in 1956. Hans added certification by PSIA to his certification by the Swiss Ski Instructors and moved with his wife Barbara to Bridgton in 1958. That first year was eventful for the Jennis and Pleasant Mountain.

This picture of Hans Jenni and his stylish form was used in silhouette as part of an area logo.

In November Jordan Marsh invited several New England ski areas to participate in their first ski show in Boston. Skiing on a 45 foot carpeted ramp in the parking lot and interviewing on a number of Boston, radio talk shows along with a TV appearance the couple garnered a great deal of publicity for the mountain to kick off the season.

In addition to directing the skischool, Hans and Barbara also ran the ski shop which was located in the basement of the lodge. Cave like, the shop was dark and had a workbench jammed under the stairs. The shop carried only necessities, goggles, gloves, hats and wax. Rental skis had bear trap bindings and adjusting them often resulted in fingers being crunched under ski boots. Spring thaw brought a stream of water running through the basement right under the service counter.

That first season Hans recruited and hired instructors by mail and as the season progressed he had a few full time local instructors and part timers on busy weekends. The Jennis' goal was to provide pupils easy and fun ways to learn to ski and the mail order instructors carried out the idea. According to Barbara Jenni, "Things went well until mid January. The entire Northeast was hit with the worst possible weather. For more than a week, Mother Nature produced rain and freezing rain. The mountain looked like a blue popsicle." She related how management tried to break up the ice with a farm harrow towed behind the snow cat, but to no avail.

She continued, "Of course, Hans had to show he could ski anything and after a trip up the main slope on the snow cat he skied down and behind him his trail looked

Hans Jenni and his wife Barbara

The East T-bar installed in 1963. Note the heavy springs which made it tough for small skiers and children to ride. Photo Credit: Bruce Cole

as if he was wearing ice skates". It eventually snowed and everyone got through the season.

At the time a group lesson was $3.00, 2 lessons $5.00 and a book of eight lessons $19.00. A private lesson was $6.00 and equipment including skis, boots, bindings, and poles ran under $100.

As the demand grew more instructors were needed and Hans began bringing over Swiss ski instructors each year. Friends were happy to house them for the season and it was great publicity that brought new energy to the area.

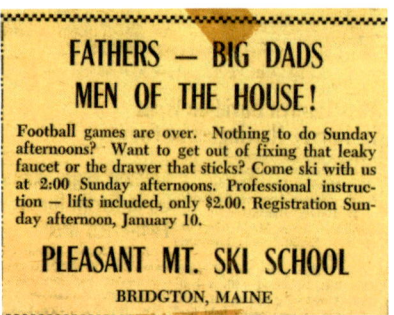 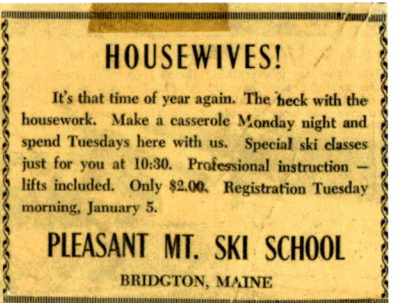

These ads were typical of those run by the Pleasant Mountain Ski Scholl during the Jenni years

As Pleasant Mountain, the ski school and shop grew, the influence of the area grew in Portland. Through the efforts of Tom Bennett, the Downeast ski Club offered a learn to ski progam at the YMCA. Hans gave a talk and exercises for two nights, with movies and door prizes followed by two on hill lessons, all for $6.00. The club did such a great job on advertising that 250 people arrived when they expected 100 at the most. The program not only attracted beginners but folks who had been skiing for awhile.

There were also special classes for Bridgton Academy and Westbrook Junior College along with classes for housewives and dads. Former Bowdoin College Ski Team Captain Bruce Chalmers ran racing classes and there were also racing camps for brand new junior skiers.

An innovative program, one of the first of its kind, was for the children at Prides Training School of South Portland. Volunteers from the Portland Junior League transported the children to the area where they were provided with equipment from the mountain and Hans and his teachers volunteered their time. Barbara Jenni remembered, "It was a very successful operation and there was not a dry eye when the children could manage the lift. Hans and his instructors received cards from the children for many years".

A Pleasant Mountain patch,

Thanks in large part to the Jennis and their ski school, the sixties were years of growth for Pleasant Mountain, but at the end of the 66-67 season management offered only a one year contract so the Jennis decided to retire and focus on their summer business, Tarry A While Resort on Highland Lake.

One weekend in the early sixties, A father purchased a private lesson from Hans Jenni's ski school. Today Chet Homer cannot say if the instructor he had that day was actually Hans, but he does recall, "He had a European accent". Certainly neither the instructor nor the pupil had any idea that 30 years later the pupil would own the ski area.

THE SEVENTIES AND EIGHT OWNERS

In 1969 Al Cooley decided that he had had enough of owning a ski area and a sale was arranged to eight Portland area businessmen led by Theodore Logan. He was joined by Ed Beaulieu, Bob Jordan, Bob Cullinan, Joe Hutchins, Dr. Davy John, Dr. Glen Hansen, and Tom Carr. Logan became president of the new group and they set out to expand Pleasant Mountain to handle the ever increasing numbers of skiers. After having the Maine ski market to themselves for the first decade and most of the second, by the late sixties, Maine now had Sunday River, Saddleback, Mt. Abram and Sugarloaf and

Many summers were spent in construction of lifts, trails, lights, snowmaking and buildings. This was erecting a tower for the Pine Slope Double Chair in 1969.

Loading Maine's first chair lift in the sixties.

lift lines were a major concern of skiers.

With two t-bars and a top to bottom double chair Pleasant Mountain had good uphill capacity for the number of trails but more was needed. The first new lift was the Pine Chair, a Stadeli Double in 1969. They also moved the Rabbit Run beginner area across the road where new skiers could be totally separated from the more advanced skiers. With their own T-bar it was a perfect teaching area at the time.

The biggest expansion by this team came in 1972. As Ted Logan described it, "We bought land to the west of the area and on Rte. 302, but we couldn't get the connecting land, so we put in the East. This increased the area in every way. A 4400 foot

This set of photos shows a Tucker Snocat with a roller used to pack fresh snow, a chain drag used to smooth the slopes with another Tucker in the background, and a Thiokol, a machine that replaced the Tuckers. This groomer had hydraulics allowing the blade seen in the front. Also notice the Powdermaker being hauled behind, a device that revolutionized grooming after its invention at Lost Valley in 1965. At the controls is Dick Andrews who handled grooming in the late seventies.

Hall double chair carried skiers to the summit and gave them a new set of trails to ski in the early morning sun. Even today, regular Shawnee Peak skiers know to start their day on the sunny slopes. They can also take their morning coffee break in the East Lodge right next to the lift's loading area. It was a complete package and vastly increased the area's ability to spread more skiers around the mountain.

In 1976, Tim Cyr, a Chevrus Grad was hired after finishing Grad School as an assistant manager and following Russ Haggett's retirement in 1978 took over as GM.

PLEASANT MOUNTAIN FREESTYLE

In the early seventies Pleasant Mountain was a hotbed for up-and-coming freestylers, several of whom went on to national prominence within a few years. Greg Stump was one of those young athletes who brought home plenty of medals, but nowadays he's best known as a producer of ski films.

Stump and his family had moved to Maine in 1968 and adopted Pleasant Mountain as their home ski area. Greg, along with his brother Geoff and sister Kim teamed up with Frank Howell to ski the mountain. Too young to join the race program they joined a new program run by Peter Pinkham, Junior Masters.

This program was based on the PSIA Final Forms, which in those days were a key part of instructor certification. Instead of racing against the clock, they were judged on how well they carved their turns and displayed the proper form to make the skis work as they were designed, but bear in mind those skis were nearly straight, not shaped to make a carve the way today's are.

Bruce "Boogie" Cole in a full layout forward flip in 1976.

In 1969 when Rudi Wyrsch arrived to direct the ski school, these kids were ready for something more than simply perfecting a turn and Wyrsch (Known as the Clown Prince of Skiing) was the perfect example. Wyrsch would ski down the mountain performing Royal Christies and other maneuvers. He would also do exhibitions of aerials, although jumping was if not forbidden, certainly frowned upon by management.

A Pleasant Mountain Ski School patch from the seventies.

Stump and Howell related how they built a jump to work on helicopters, a jump where the skier rotates 360 degrees before landing. As they did this after the lifts closed they built the jump just above the lodge so they could see by the lights of the building. Following Russ Haggett's retirement Ron Kutcowicz became GM and he was not only more tolerant of the jumping but actually encouraged the young skiers.

A jump was built by chair lift tower 13 (the bump just above today's mid station on the summit chair) where they could jump without getting into trouble as long as they confined it to that one spot. According to Stump, this worked fine until one of their group tried an inverted maneuver and once again management got nervous.

The junior masters program was also growing at other mountains and in 1972 the Maine State Ski Masters circuit was developed
giving the skiers an opportunity to compete against other teams in the state. Bruce Cole had returned from Aspen to teach and direct the program and the Pleasant Mountain team traveled around the state and over to New Hampshire for competitions.

While the juniors had their Masters, Bernie Weischel who operates the Boston Ski Show and others had started the Chevy Pro Freestyle Tour starring the likes of Wayne Wong and John Clen-

Ted Logan presenting the 1973 President's Cup Jeff Coffin. The trophy was supposed to be retired to the three time winner, but Coffin said it remained on display in the bar where it was destroyed in the 1983 fire. The plate with the names was all that was salvaged and it was on the wall in the rental shop for many years.

The famous donuts being prepared in the kitchen by Louie Dagel in 1973.

denin. In one of his events at Waterville Valley, Greg who was 13 or 14 at the time presented himself to Weischel as Bruce Cole's agent and some how convinced the tour director that Cole should be allowed to compete even though he was unseeded. In the qualifiers Cole beat Wong, Clendenin and other top competitors to get into the finals. Unfortunately he bombed in the finals, but the Pleasant Mountain skiers had made an impact.

As the Masters transformed into freestyle through the seventies the Pleasant Mountain skiers progressed and in 1978 they made a road trip by van to Copper Mountain in Colorado for the National Championships. Unfortunately, Howell was hit hard by the altitude, (Copper is 9600 feet at the base and climbs close to 12,000 at the summit, quite a change for skiers living close to sea level.), and it was serious. He had to be transported to Denver and hospitalized. Greg and Frank were and are best of friends who described themselves as archrivals.

That left the rest of the team to compete and they brought home the medals. Peter Young finished first overall and Greg Stump was second, first in his junior class. Geoff Stump finished first in his age group as did Doug Rand of Westbrook. In all the Pleasant Mountain skiers brought home six national titles and in later competition Frank Howell got his share, finally totaling six himself.

In those days, freestyle was not an Olympic sport, but these Pleasant Mountain skiers were the forerunners and they put Pleasant Mountain on the national freestyle map.

OPENING THE 1978-79 SEASON

This appeared in a ski supplement to the Maine Sunday Telegram under my by-line in the fall of 1978.

Last year Pleasant Mountain celebrated its 40th season and did it while making a healthy profit. That alone is enough for a celebration in the ski industry.

This year's visitors to Maine's largest commuter mountain will find a number of significant changes.

A pin from the eighties

Probably the most important is the speeding up of Maine's oldest chair lift. The main chair has been rebuilt making it possible to reduce the length of the ride to eight minutes.

This will open up the whole mountain to weekday skiers and shorten the lines at the base. The change also increases the uphill capacity to 4300 skiers per hour, second only to Sugarloaf in Maine.

The rest of the improvements have been made with bulldozers, dynamite and hay. Over 20 cases of dynamite were used in the East Area, making it possible to ski the Appalachian run full width. It's hoped this will spread the crowd, further reducing lift lines on the other lifts.

Haggett's and the Pine Slope have also been groomed and widened and the freestylers will find a new jump that is the best in the country.

New this year also will be the coming of Carroll Reed to the ski shop.

Some things remain the same. The mountain hasn't grown so the vertical drop is still just over 1250 feet. Tim Cyr remains area manager, Dick Andrews will continue his snow farming as mountain manager and Roz Manwaring will direct the ski school.

Bruce Cole will direct the area's very successful freestyle program and those huge donuts, baked right at the mountain will still be available while they last in the cafeteria. Pleasant Mountain skiers consume some 1500 of them each morning.

Pleasant offers 20 miles of slopes and trails with a lot of open slope skiing. Uphill capacity is provided by three chairlifts and three T-bars.

The area is known for weekday business when there's plenty of skiing and no crowds.

Best deals; Tuesday and Thursday, lift ticket, lesson and lunch all for $7.00. Wednesdays, same deal including your favorite beverage in the Loft Lounge for $8.00.

NEW OWNERS FOLLOWING THE NO SNOW WINTER

The no snow winter

The winter or non-winter of 1979-80 played a major role in the history of Pleasant Mountain for both the eight owners and their young GM Tim Cyr. Following the strong season of the previous year there was plenty of reason to be optimistic and everything was in place for the first snow. But it didn't snow. It didn't snow in December, or January, or February. Finally, the snow came in early March and the area opened March 11th. For one week! That was it. What little snow fell after that was not enough to open and the season was over.

Following the near snowless winter of 1979-1980, the Portland Eight decided it was time to sell and in the fall of 1981, a new Pleasant Mountain Corp. purchased the area. The main principals were Peter Dromeshauser of Dedham, Mass. and Jerry Funzel of Morristown, NJ and Davis Dunn, former mountain manager at Vail, Co came on as GM.

The new owners made a commitment to install snowmaking and have it operational by Christmas. Work on the new system began immediately with plans to cover the East Slope, Main and Pines from mid station on the main chair down, three slopes serviced by four lifts.

While the short time frame prevented covering more of the area that fall, pumps

New for 1984 Top to Bottom Snowmaking

Ski the sensible alternative!
Fun for the entire family, yet big and exciting!

Pleasant Mountain offers the entire family an exciting and most affordable ski experience. The recently installed large snowmaking complex, and with this year's expansion to the summit, insures snow cover from late November to mid-April. And with a fleet of modern grooming equipment working constantly, you'll find the best conditions possible whatever the weather.

Pleasant Mountain continues with its philosophy of giving all family members the best skiing experience in a friendly atmosphere. This year, ski Maine's sensible alternative...SKI PLEASANT MOUNTAIN

- 1256' vertical rise
- 6 lifts
- 23 slopes & trails
- snowmaking top to bottom

- limited tickets
- learn to ski program
- recreational racing

- daily grooming
- ski school
- ski shops
- day care

Big, beautiful... and affordable.

Within easy driving distance:
38 miles from Portland, Maine
For lodging information: (207)647-2604

18 miles from North Conway, N.H.
140 miles from Boston, Mass.

Pleasant Mountain

Snow conditions call: (207)647-8444

Route 302, Bridgton, Maine 04009

Reader Service No. 4

This ad introduced top to bottom snowmaking at the beginning of the 1983-84 season.

The dining room with a view of the slopes.

and water source were set up to eventually service the entire mountain. They made the deadline and by Christmas the guns were blowing snow but it really didn't matter. Mother Nature provided abundant snow that winter and the season could have progressed without the manmade variety, but the snow guns were used to insure a good base in case the weather changed.

Ads that fall touted, "New Management", "Snowmaking" and lift tickets $6.00 midweek, $12.00 weekends.

Dunn left after that season and Ed Rock was hired to replace him. Rock had previously been mountain manager at Okemo in Vermont. Under this management team, a new nursery was built, the base lodge renovated, and new grooming equipment acquired. And the ad to begin the 1983-84 season proclaimed, "Top to Bottom Snowmaking".

The renovation of the base lodge was actually necessitated by a fire Labor Day weekend that destroyed the entire upper floor of the East wing of the lodge. According to Ed Rock, an outdoor concert was scheduled that weekend which had to be canceled. The fire started in the electrical works in the kitchen around 2-3 AM and was called in by someone who saw it. Ed, who was living in Alpine Village (A group of second homes below Mountain Road a short way off rte. 302) at the time, arrived about 4 AM, along with the fire department. He noted that they did a great job saving the rest of the building. The extensive smoke and water damage was cleaned up and the new Blizzard's Pub rebuilt on the top floor, with everything up and running by mid December, before the start of the new season.

The dining room wing after the fire.

In 1984 a new owner joined the team. Dave Lubrano's history in the area dated back to his camping at Winona across the lake from Pleasant Mountain. His key role was to provide financing a new chair lift. That summer Maine's first chair lift was replaced by a summit triple. Once again the project continued well into the fall as Ed Rock, related, "We flew the concrete for the lift tower bases on Halloween." It was tight but the new lift was in place to start the season, it shortened both the ride up and the lift lines. That same year lake front condos were developed on land the company had sold to a separate developer below Mountain Road. According to Chet Homer, "Dave Lubrano was the most loyal of any of the former owners and to this day the Lubrano children, spouses and grandchildren remain devoted Shawnee Peak skiers".

Unfortunately, the hastily installed snowmaking had some problems and in 1984, 2000 feet of pipe froze and a major overhaul was needed. Ed Rock, remembered, "We ripped everything out, built a new upper pump house and he had 50,000 feet of pipe in the parking lot." The weather didn't cooperate as heavy rains hit that summer and into the fall. Skidders were on the mountain trying to pull pipe through the mud. The mountain got open on limited terrain, but snowmaking didn't commence until January 11.
By then a group of season pass holders in the Knight's Hill development called a meeting and asked the mountain to explain. Wendy McInerny, marketing and PR that year, along with Ed Rock faced the skiers and explained how the weather was the culprit. After mid January season pass holders and day skiers alike learned how much more snow the new system could blow across the slopes and the rest of the season went well.

The next two winters were uneventful, and in 1987 Peter Dromeshauser put the ski area on the market.

The mountain as it appeared with lights across Moose Pond, a major step forward.

ALPINE SLIDE

To begin the summer of 1982, in order to expand summer business, Pleasant Mountain installed an Alpine Slide. The same ride was successfully operating at Attitash in the Mount Washington Valley, but it was not to be in Bridgton. While the both the White Mountains and Bridgton's Lake Region were filled with tourists in the summer there was a key difference. Those in the mountains were looking for a mountain experience, while those on the lakes were there to enjoy the water. On the warm sunny days they stayed on the water and only left when it rained, a time when the slide could not operate safely. The Alpine Slide operated one more summer in 1983 and the following summer was sold to Vernon Valley (Now Mountain Creek) ski area in New Jersey.

The short lived Alpine Slide.

SHAWNEE GROUP

In 1988, Pleasant Mountain got its fourth owner and a name change. The Shawnee Group, operator of Shawnee Mountain in Pennsylvania purchased the mountain and renamed it Shawnee Peak. Naturally, locals and long time Pleasant Mountain skiers resisted the change, but the new owners wasted no time in making significant improvements and one is a key factor in the success of the operation today.

The first year saw the lighting of 60 % of the terrain, with state of the art hydrogen lights from mid station down and a new double chair for beginners as that area was moved back on the mountain side of the road. The next year in 1989, lights were extended to the summit making Shawnee Peak the largest night skiing operation in New England, a distinction it holds to this day. This act provided the area with a niche that would prove critical to success then and years into the future. Before long Shawnee Peak was servicing close to 4000 school age kids a week and adult racing leagues were keeping things humming evenings. The improvements totaled over $2 million.

While Ed Rock remained as manager two key positions were filled from Pennsylvania. Brian Hendricks took over as ski school director and Bernie Vigna moved into the ski patrol director's position.

The expanded ski day under the lights required an expansion of ski school as lessons increased to 2000 a week. Naturally that meant an increase in the number of instructors and 75 were brought on to start the 1989 season with a goal of having 100 by the year's end.

Vigna took over a ski patrol with six full time paid and six part time paid and about 40 volunteers. Vigna noted that while his new mountain was more demanding than what he left behind in Pennsylvania there was much less first aid to perform. This was attributed to the higher level of skiers at the Maine area. Hendricks echoed that sentiment from a ski school standpoint, observing that the level of skiers here was much higher than in Pennsylvania. He explained that a typical group of 80 skiers in Pennsylvania would be made up of 20 skiers and 60 beginners, while here the ratio is reversed.

Both had good things to say about the folks who frequent Shawnee Peak at Pleasant Mountain. According to Hendricks, "Skiers are a lot nicer here. We used to see people carry their city pace into the lodge and onto the hill. Here, it's more relaxed. At 8:30 when the lifts open, there's no one in line. We get very few complaints."

Under the Shawnee Group business at the area increased with the popularity of night skiing, the school groups and night racing. But after six years, the company, facing financial difficulties decided to sell the Maine operation.

HAGGETT MEMORIAL FUND

Following Russ Haggett's death in 1991, the Downeast Ski Club wanted to recognize Haggett and his contribution to skiing and his work in the community. Knowing his devotion to the local youth and how he had always made sure any kid who wanted to ski got to whether they had the money or not, it was decided the most appropriate way to honor him would be a scholarship fund. In March of 1992, three months into the drive, club Member don Wyman reported that close to $7000 had been raised towards their goal of $10,000, assuring $500 to a senior that year.

The first annual Russ Haggett Memorial Race had drawn 117 skiers the last week in February who contributed $605 to the fund. The racers were a combination of day skiers and families who grew up at Pleasant Mountain. Working on the race were Downeast Ski Clubbers and ski area employees. It was the kind of team effort that was typical of the Haggett years, effort that is alive and well at Shawnee Peak.

Since its startup in 1992, the Russ Haggett Memorial Fund has grown and the race continues to be a key part of keeping it alive and growing. Tom Bennett credited Shawnee's June Gyger with playing a key role along with members of the ski patrol, mountain workers and volunteers to making the race an annual success. From starting with a single scholarship for $500, the fund has grown to supply two scholarships for $500, to the past ten years

Russ Haggett, area manager for 32 years.

of giving two $1000 scholarships to graduates of Lake Region High School each year. Tom's mention of June Gyger brings to light another key aspect of Shawnee Peak's success. June is one of several employees who have been with the mountain for three plus decades. She started as a member of the ski patrol in 1979 and patrolled as a volunteer until 1988. After a brief stint working for Phil and Marlis Libby at the Sports Haus, Henry Hudson asked her to be race secretary for the mountain and she continued until her retirement in 2016, organizing races and making sure they run smoothly. For the last 22 years her son Danny Gyger has been performing the outside work on races while June handles things inside, collecting fees, registering the participants, runnin g the timing, and tabulating the results.

It's a big job with the mountain hosting high school, Maine Alpine Racing Assn., USSA, and corporate races in addition to charity events, as many as 75 races annually. As it is with any ski area hosting races requires a significant commitment from the ski area in terms of equipment, snowmaking, grooming and man hours. In addition to area personnel, volunteers are needed to serve as gatekeepers, race officials, timing, course maintenance, registration, and tabulating results.

CHET HOMER AND THE MODERN ERA

When, after five years of ownership, the Shawnee Group put their Maine ski area on the market the question was who would buy it. That year 1993 was early in the consolidation of ski areas that would continue through the rest of the nineties. SKI, the parent company of Killington had acquired Mount Snow, Waterville Valley, and Sugarloaf and Les Otten who had Sunday River at its peak was in the process of acquiring Sugarbush. There was plenty of speculation about these and others in the ski industry, but it turned out to be a Maine businessman with no ties to the industry other than he liked sports and skiing in particular.

The latest of pins for Shawnee Peak.

Chet Homer, who had taken that private lesson some 30 years before at Pleasant Mountain, heard rumors of the sale and in the spring of 1994, he contacted the management of the Shawnee Group and told them he would like to arrange a meeting and bring along his banker. The idea that a potential buyer would bring along his banker told them that this was a serious candidate for a purchase and the meeting was set up.

The deal was closed and in 1994 Shawnee Peak at Pleasant Mountain had a new owner, setting the stage for a period of improvement that continues today. Homer brought a solid business background to his new endeavor. He was the number two man at Tom's of Maine, Executive Vice President and Chief Financial Officer, and Vice Chairman of the Board of Ocean National Bank in Kennebunk.

Asked why, with his financial background, he would enter the ski business, he replied, "I always wanted to be my own boss and sports and recreation were my main interests."

As to why Shawnee Peak in particular he knew exactly what was needed, "The number one requirement for a successful ski area is water and snowmaking. The Shawnee Group had invested in the lights so everything was in place. Also, I was comfortable with Ed Rock and his team". Thirteen mile long Moose Pond at the foot of the mountain provided water for snowmaking that any ski area would envy and the investments had been made under previous owners to cover the entire mountain.

But the new owner was not satisfied with the status quo and never would be as his record of improvements in the years since demonstrates. He went down to Seven Springs, the very successful Pennsylvania resort to learn first hand about snowmaking and other aspects of running a ski resort. In one of his first moves to improve skiing for the ticket buyers, afternoon grooming was introduced so the night skiers would find the same pristine corduroy early morning skiers experienced.

A Kassbohrer PistenBully snowcat, part of the current fleet blading away the moguls.

The first big investment came the next summer when in 1995, Chet and Ed went to Hazen McMullen, then president of Kassbohrer and bought three brand new PistenBully snow cats. McMullen told Ed, "If you take care of them, you'll have them a long time." Some areas lease groomers, but Chet likes to own them and his GM agreed. It's also important to do business with Kassbohrer. Originally it was Valley Engineering that imported the German machines, but the manufacturer bought out the company and moved from Gray to Lewiston. Rock emphasized the importance of that proximity, "We can call for a part at 8 PM and pick it up at midnight".

Rock gave a lot credit for the longevity of the big snow cats to his mechanic, Kenny Cohen of Fryeburg. Cohen has been with first Pleasant Mountain and now Shawnee Peak for 40 plus years, another example of the kind of loyalty that a number of Shawnee employees have demonstrated. While his employment at Shawnee is seasonal, his work as a mechanic on heavy equipment was year round. As soon as the area closed each spring Cohen would go to work for Pike Industries to keep their big machines operating smoothly through the construction season. He recently retired from Pike, but still keeps Shawnee Peak's grooming machines running smoothly.

After three years of careful planning, Shawnee Peak entered the season prepared to celebrate birthday number 60 with an ad that announced, "WE'RE MAKING HISTORY, WITH THE LARGEST EXPANSION PROJECT IN 60 YEARS". The area entered the 1997-1998 season with a new quad chair servicing the Pine Slope and adjacent trails, a new triple chair for the East area, and a surface lift at the base, a 40 % increase in uphill capacity. Snowmaking was expanded and the ad concluded, "As Always, New England's Largest Night Skiing Facility".

The quad serving the Pine Slope and trails to the west virtually eliminated lift lines except for brief times when ski school classes were heading up for the beginning of classes. Even on the busiest days skiers would seldom spend more than few minutes in line for a run. Over in the East area, the triple had a similar effect on lines.

Then Governor Angus King launching the new Pine Slope Quad Chair in 1997-98, Owner Chet Homer is at right.

The following year, 7000 feet of new snowmaking pipe were laid to increase capacity, and in another first the mountain installed HKD tower guns, to increase efficiency and guarantee better early season cover. The company also made its first move into lodging with the acquisition of the Shawnee Peak House. With a capacity to house 45 skiers, the house made a good choice for groups.

The first five years of the new century were fairly uneventful. School programs continued and Racing With the Moon kept pace making for busy nights and a thriving business in Blizzard's Pub. Of course, the pub for years with Steve behind the bar and now Patty has been a friendly gathering spot for years, afternoon's and evenings, kind of Maine's version of that TV bar "where everyone knows your name." On sunny days the hospitality extends to the deck and patio below.

In 2006, a major step forward in Lodging was made when a group of Portland season pass holders took on the construction of 32 two bedroom condos at the base of the East Slope. This $10 million dollar project created true ski in-ski

Skiers riding the new chair.

out lodging a mere 200 hundred yards from the base lodge and an even shorter run to the summit triple, the first on the mountain.

The development was another indication of the involvement of skiers in the resort and the return of one family as investors. Mike Keeley and Mark Hutchins partnered in the building of the condos, both long time pass holders along with their families. Hutchins is the son of Joe Hutchins, one of the Portland Eight group that owned the area through the seventies.

Mark told how his father had bought Russ Haggett's share while the others bought the remaining shares. He also related how his grandfather who owned Hutchins Trucking in South Portland gave the family its first taste of skiing at Pleasant Mountain. After purchasing a piece of land on County Road he bought three roadside cabins on Rte. One, south of Portland, transported them to the mountain on one of the company flatbeds, and hitched them together for the family's first place on the mountain.

He and his three siblings all skied out of the place on County Road where they had a trail to get them to the base area and another to get them back. His faith in the future of Shawnee Peak is demonstrated by the investment in the condos. He summed it up regarding Chet Homer, "Nobody has made a more positive contribution to the area. He's always fine tuning and he doesn't half do it. He does it right."

The condo development was well received in spite of a downturn in real estate at the time. All of the units have been sold.

The new condos built in 2006 at the base of the East Slope.

On the mountain a new trail was cut circling to the west from the summit. Sunset Boulevard was aptly named as it provided great sunset views of Mount Washington. It also gave novices an easy way off the top of the mountain, enhancing their experience as they worked their way up the ladder of skiing skills. A new groomer was added to the fleet and the East Lodge got a new wine bar. The following summer, in preparation for the 70th Anniversary, more tower guns were added along with a new pump bringing capacity to just under 4000 gallons a minute, part of the ongoing commitment of ownership to make the snowmaking more efficient while providing as much skiing as possible in the early season.

Over the years the base lodge had seen a number of enlargements and renovations, but the actual capacity had not increased for some years. That changed in 2008 with the construction of the Great Room. This 40 by 40 foot addition extended out toward the slopes in the center of the lodge. Its south facing walls of glass introduced solar heating to the lodge and helped to heat not only the new space but the entire base lodge.

The summer of 2010 brought another first to Shawnee Peak and a major change in lifts. A new triple chair replaced the summit triple with more spacious seats and more importantly, Maine's first conveyor loading. This loading system, which guaranteed skiers would be in proper position to load, allowed higher lift speeds and reduced the frequency of skier problems while loading. The combination of higher speeds and fewer stoppages increased the capacity of the lift, again reducing lift lines.

THE ICE STORM

Weather is often at the heart of tough times at ski areas, but it's usually warm rains and thaws that are thought of as the worst that can happen. But January 9, 1998 brought something far worse, freezing rain. The ice storm hit all of New England and parts of Quebec, wreaking havoc throughout the region. It brought down power lines and in places power was out for weeks. Others lost power for only a matter of hours, but Bridgton, was one of the towns where the power loss extended for days after other communities got the lights back on. That January, it took ten days to get power back to Shawnee Peak and Martin Luther King weekend was lost, always a key piece of any ski area's economic pie.

Even if power had been restored the day after the storm, the mountain could not have operated. Trees were bent over or down and light lines had been taken down by the weight of an inch or more of ice. Ed Rock through his contacts with the folks at Shawnee in Pennsylvania, found crews he could call in to perform the cleanup and reconnect the power lines around the mountain. It was a big job, crews with chain saws had to remove trees and limbs from trails, while others worked in the air on light towers and lift towers to remove hanging branches and reconnect the lines. Ed recalled, "We fed everybody with barbecues because of the lack of power."

By the time Central Maine Power Co. had restored power to the area, the outside crews and the mountain team at Shawnee Peak had things ready to go again and the winter of 98 continued, but no one would ever forget that massive ice storm

January 16 Ed Rock sent the following memo to all employees

As you are aware, this past week's ice storm has been one of record proportions. The damage to trees, light lines, poles, and lifts is visually obvious, let alone the loss of operating revenue. All of this is particularly frustrating after a great start to the ski season over Christmas vacation.

These photos demonstrate the extreme damage left by the 1998 ice storm.

    Despite all of these negatives referred to above, one very positive element has been the tremendous effort put forth by many Shawnee Peak employees. From Friday (January 9th) thru the present time, numerous employees have been working long hours, clearing brush, preparing the snowmaking system, and assisting in the repair of the light lines. Immediately after the storm, certain employees took the initiative to come to work to offer their help in any way that would benefit our recovery. Lift operators, snowmakers, maintenance, groomers, patrol, and other personnel concentrated on the mountain, with support provided by building/grounds, office and food/beverage. A few examples of such effort and caring were employees having to "cut their way" into work; bringing their own chain saws and gear to work each day: or volunteering to drive additional distances to pick up fellow employees or needed material required to get the job done. But perhaps the most impressive, was that despite each of these employees personal situation (no power or heat, phone outage, family matters, and damage to personal property) these people made the commitment to work at Shawnee Peak each day. Through their efforts much has been accomplished despite difficult and sometimes dangerous situations.

Through all of these employees' efforts, the mountain is rapidly getting back to normal day to day operations. Having been in the ski industry for many years, I have never seen such dedicated and hard working people. To list all of these employees names is not possible, but hopefully after a period of time their identities will become known. If possible, please extend your gratitude to these individuals who have put our mountain back together.

The ice storm was picked up and covered nationally by CNN. Chet Homer, in just his fourth year of ownership was at the winter trade conference in Vermont in the middle of the outage and gained some insight into the character of the industry he had joined. "I got offers of support and equipment from many owners. The ski industry is very close and that was very comforting back then and still part of the industry' today."

THE MODERN SKI SCHOOL

Recent years have seen dramatic changes in teaching newbies to ski and Scott Condon was a key part of the Shawnee Ski School during these critical years. An avid skier who worked as a golf pro in his home town of Kennebunkport in the summer, he decided to put his teaching skills to work as an instructor and in 1989 joined the ski school at Shawnee Peak. In 1995 he moved into the position of director of that ski school a post he held until 2009 when he moved into group sales. Now a full time employee Scott has been with the company 28 years.

Asked about the biggest change in teaching the sport he was quick to answer, "Shaped skis. Before, with the long skis we would struggle to get skiers up the lift. It would take 45 minutes and sometimes a full two hours of climbing a short hill and skiing back down before they had sufficient skill to go up the lift. With the shorter shaped skis beginners quickly learned to turn and control their speed."

An instructor one on one with a snowboarder.

Shaped skis were another example of how the owner was willing to invest in making a better experience for all skiers, especially newcomers. More recently Shawnee Peak has invested in the latest technology, "Rockered skis" which makes learning even easier. The entire rental fleet has this new technology.

Condon arrived as an instructor the season after the lights were installed and recalled how the ski school was "slammed with school kids" for hour after hour with groups of 6-8. At the time the school had 175 instructors, with 8 full time.

The origins of that junior program can be found in the work of a volunteer in the early sixties. Bruce Chalmers a volunteer coach of the Bridgton High Girls ski team wanted to get as many kids as possible on skis so he contacted various area schools and convinced them to bus kids to Pleasant Mountain for an afternoon of skiing. By recruiting instructors, (Also volunteers), helpers with the buses and in the base lodge, Chalmers grew the program to as many as 400 kids. It was the forerunner of today's expansive junior programs at Shawnee Peak.

A skier practicing his skills in the half pipe.

A ski instructor one on one with a skier.

Among his memories was the invasion by snowboarders. That craze caught ski areas everywhere by surprise and Shawnee Peak was no exception. In 1989 they had one snowboard instructor and three rental snowboards. All of a sudden half of the lesson requests were for snowboards. It reached a point where a learning snowboarder who showed exceptional promise was offered a job teaching others on weekends.

The first half pipe in 1991-92 had to be bulldozed and was replaced with the first terrain park in which skiers were not allowed. That has all changed today with the advent of twin tip skis and events such as the X-Games. According to Condon, lessons are now about 70 % ski and 30 % snowboard. He feels it's mostly because skiing is easier to learn.

Now Condon, a retired PSIA Level III instructor, is handling group sales and IT duties and a modern ski school with the latest in equipment hums along with programs for all ages of skiers and riders, Condon summed up his reason for being there 28 years, "We all do whatever needs to be done. We're a tight little family here."

THE MODERN SKI PATROL

When Maine's first ski patrol served Pleasant Mountain in the early years it met the standards and needs of the day. Most ski areas operated with primarily volunteer patrols which worked with nearly all of the business on weekends with an occasional holiday. A typical area the size of Pleasant Mountain would hire a professional patroller to work mid week and leave the weekends and even the organization of the patrol to the volunteers. By the seventies that was changing. Many ski areas were becoming ski resorts and offering vacation packages and mid week business was growing. Volunteers were no longer the answer and a core of professionals was needed.

One professional had not only grown up skiing the mountain, but in 1963 broke his leg and was treated on the slope by Jimmy Jones and Bob Fitzimmons. In 1974 Henry Hudson signed on as a pro patrolman and in 1979 he became patrol director. In those days of limited patrol budgets there was no money for such luxuries as radios. Accidents and other instances where patrol attentions were needed were reported to lift attendants at the base and the request phoned to members stationed at the summit. Hudson arranged to trade season passes with David Libby for five radios and communication became much more efficient.

In 1985 Ed Rock called and asked Henry to add the race program to his duties. June Gyger was directing the program inside and in the timing shack, and someone was needed to run things on the mountain. Hudson continued with both programs until he retired from patrolling in 1998 and the race program a year later. In 1978 Sonny Davis who had patrolled in Colorado joined the Pleasant Mountain patrol as a volunteer. In the early eighties he moved into the Bridgton area to work as an electrician and became a professional patroller at the mountain.

Since 2000 he has been directing the patrol which has grown both in size and skills. When Jimmy Jones started that first ski patrol all those years ago all that was required was 26 hours of training through a Red Cross first aid course. Today's patrol members complete an Outdoor Emergency Care course which is closer to 80 hours. Add in CPR and an annual refresher course plus on hill training in handling rescue toboggans and today's patroller is light years ahead of those early patrollers. The lights at Shawnee Peak add another dimension to patrolling. The need to cover those extra hours requires more members and regular shift assignments to assure coverage. Today's patrol has as many as 80 volunteers and 10 professionals

An example of Shawnee Patrol members following the leadership tradition of Maine's first ski patrol so many years ago is Tom Gyger. As the first aid training evolved through a more comprehensive Red Cross program and on into the current OEC training Gyger not only headed up the training at Shawnee Peak but as advisor for the entire Maine Region of the National Ski Patrol. His work earned a service award from NSP, but also election to the Maine Ski Hall of Fame in 2014.

Schedules have to be carefully worked out to cover not only weekends and midweek but nights as well. Their duties are more than simply being on hand to care for injured skiers. They are the on hill eyes and ears of management. Duties include checking trails, safety gates on lifts, watching over lift lines and answering questions from skiers. Correct signage is a responsibility ranging from trail closings to caution signs.

One of Davis proudest achievements is the creation and maintaining of a special student program. The National Ski Patrol did away with their junior program some years ago, but he could see the benefits and with Doug Wall, a retired school teacher set up a program whereby students could start at age 15. The first year they receive a discount ticket and ski with the patrol learning procedures. If they show the interest and ability, they take the OEC course and proceed to ski and toboggan training. These young patrollers wear a blue vest until age 18, at which time they are awarded the red jacket of the Shawnee Peak patrol. They also receive high school credits for the program. The program has been recognized by the National Ski Patrol and is being used as a model by other ski areas around the country.

The mountain as seen by approaching skiers in the evening.

MOONLIGHT CHARITY CHALLENGE

During the first three years of his owner ship Chet Homer said he had the most fun in 1996, the first year of the Moonlight Charity Challenge, a benefit run for the Jimmy Fund and the area's own Adaptive Skiing Program. They brought in Paul Hurley a noted fund raising specialist from Boston for the event and the results were spectacular. Hurley brought in Wayne Wong and TV Personalities including Dennis Haskins, who played a high school principal on the TV series, "Saved by the Bell". to create an attraction and, using his contacts with American Airlines, Hurley recruited a team of flight attendants to sell raffle tickets. They not only sold them at the event but somehow got permission to sell them at both Logan Airport in Boston and O'Hare in Chicago. What guy sitting at a bar could resist when one of these lovely blondes appeared at his elbow with a fistful of raffle tickets. They called themselves the "Fabulous Raffle Babes" and their work at Blizzard's Pub was very fruitful. The event raised close to $50,000 that year, setting a high bar for future events.

In its fifth year, the Challenge was run for the benefit of the Ronald MacDonald House in Portland and the Adaptive Program. The teams of skiers, through pledges and raffle ticket sales raised $30,000 that year and in the ensuing years the event has grown to a point where the totals raised the last two years were $50,000 and $75,000.

Melissa Rock joined the Shawnee Peak team as director of marketing and PR in 2001 and remembered how the volunteers from Camp Sunshine showed up in large numbers. Since that time, Camp Sunshine had been the major beneficiary along with the Adaptive Program and every year as many as 200 turn out to assist with the fund raiser. The camp is so well known across the state and beyond that teams turn out for the Challenge, making it one of the biggest events of the season.

Camp Sunshine is a year-round retreat, which provides respite, support, joy and hope to children with life-threatening illnesses and their immediate families through various stages of a child's illness.

The program is free of charge to all families, and includes 24-hour onsite medical and psychosocial support. Bereavement groups are also offered for families who have lost a child to an illness.

Matt Hoidal, Executive Director explained Camp Sunshine's involvement in the Moonlight Charity Challenge, "We always try to be a contributor and not just a taker. We have such broad support, that we can get teams to take part in the event. Shawnee Peak has been great. In the nine years we have been involved, they have raised over $250,000 for the camp. It has helped fund our winter programs."

The most recent benefactor of the Challenge has been the Maine Children's Cancer Program. Program Director Elizabeth Murray said the thousands raised by the Moonlight Charity Challenge for the last ten years has been a key factor in the success of the program, "Without those dollars raised our program would not exist".

While the funding is critical, Murray cited an equally important contribution by Shawnee Peak, "We receive free family passes for patients and families of those in our program. This allows them to go out on the mountain and ski as a family, it's so life affirming, such a healthy outdoor activity."

Once each season all of the families on treatment gather at Shawnee Peak for day of skiing. It's a pairing of families and clinicians on the mountain, out of the clinic setting. There are as many as 25 families in the program at any given time. Murray called it a truly therapeutic event and noted, "All of this is due to the passion of Chet Homer. He has made possible this benefit to our program."

In just over 20 years, Shawnee Peak skiers through the Moonlight Charity Challenge have raised over $650,000 to benefit a variety of charities. Another example of the commitment to helping others is the January ski day for the Boys and Girls Club of Dorchester. It started in 2011, with 150 kids treated to a day of skiing, with all expenses including transportation covered by Shawnee Peak and continues to this day.

Part of the team brought together for the Moonlight Charity Challenge, L-R: Chet Homer, Dennis Haskins, Paul Hurley, Shirley Homer and Wayne Wong.

ADAPTIVE SKIING PROGRAM

One program at Shawnee Peak flies under the radar, primarily because it operates mostly midweek mornings, thus limiting visibility to afternoon, evening or weekend skiers.. It's also an example of the foresight of Chet Homer. Within the first year of his ownership, he set up a 501 C 3 for the Adaptive Skiing Program, making all donations tax deductible and allowing volunteers to also reap the benefits of tax deductions for their contributions.

A key figure in running the programs is Ross Graham. He had started as an instructor for the regular ski school in 1991 and in his words, "When the people in ski school and group sales were looking for someone to run the program I kind of volunteered". Twenty-six years later he is still on the job working a program that runs each season from the second week in January to the first week in March.

Executive Director Charles Scribner said, "We're kind of co-directors. Ross handles school groups and works with their group leaders. I assign the volunteers and lead fund raising efforts."

In all groups from 14 schools and communities are involved including Lake Region High School, Fryeburg Academy, Westbrook, Windham, Poland, Portland and Bridgton. As many as 100 kids and adults attend the seven week program at a cost of $50 each for the season. That covers instruction and use of the facilities in the rustic little building just west of the base lodge which is also used by Skiwee afternoons and weekends. Rental equipment and lift tickets are donated by the mountain. The program relies mostly on teachers who come with the kids from the schools and volunteers.

Dot Robinson and friends Taken in 1999, this picture demonstrates true loyalty of three Shawnee Peak at Pleasant Mountain skiers. Left to right, Gladys Elkins of Westbrook, Dorothy "Dot" Robinson, South Portland and Lois Swindells, Hampton, NH. All three skied regularly at the area into their eighties and Dot skied until age 94.five years before her death in 2011 at age 99. When it was announced that in lieu of flowers donations should be made to the Shawnee Peak Adaptive Skiing Program, fellow skiers, friends and especially Downeast Ski Club members donated some $2000 enough to purchase a sit ski for the program.

Graham has seen kids who started in grade school, skied in the program in high school and are now coming as adults. It takes as many instructors or trainers and aids to work with the athletes as attend each session. Most instruction is one on one with some taking two volunteers to work with a single athlete. Ross, says "My hat's off to the teachers who work with the kids in schools, at the mountain and back in the schools."

Highlights of the season are the annual Special Olympics and the arrival of kids and families from Camp Sunshine. Camp Sunshine actually brings kids and families for two sessions each winter. The families are set up with bag lunches which they can eat on the way to the mountain. Anyone who needs lessons gets them and rental equipment where way to the mountain. Anyone who needs lessons gets them and rental equipment where needed.

Matt Hoidal, Executive Director of Camp Sunshine had high praise for the staff and volunteers at the mountain, "They meet us in the parking lot. When we pull in, staff and volunteers are right there to make it seamless as we go through rentals and onto the mountain." He noted how the same people are there each year and how they remember the group and take care of their needs.

Five years ago Charlie Scribner became executive director. Scribner serves double duty, working directly with the program and as a member of the Board of Directors. According to Graham, Scribner is a valuable asset as a fund raiser, putting on the Moose Pond ½ Marathon and 5K race at Shawnee Peak each November to raise money for the program.. His ski school experience comes into play as he works with coaches and volunteers to make the groups more comfortable with their skiing experience.

Whether it's taking care of special groups such as Camp Sunshine, the Special Olympics, or their own participants, the staff and volunteers involved with the Shawnee Peak Adaptive Program have demonstrated their dedication and efficiency for nearly two decades. Ross Graham cited the contributions of the ski area, "The staff always back us up."

MOUNTAIN DEW VERTICAL CHALLENGE

On a Saturday in early February in 1992, Shawnee Peak chalked up another first. Frank Tansey who handles special events for Pepsi, was introducing a new event called the Mountain Dew race series and the very first event was held at Shawnee Peak. The race is open to everyone, with age and sex categories from kids to 80 plus. The exact numbers are not available for that first year, but the event has grown to include dozens of ski areas each ski season and a season ending finals for the winners of the various categories at the different ski areas.

Mountain Dew race day.

There are even skiers who follow the series around New England all season long in hopes of qualifying for the finals. The race is free and there are hundreds of prizes and awards following the race. Ed Rock said that skiers start signing up on race day as early as 7 AM and a typical day draws 300-400 to Shawnee Peak. They even get 300 on a rainy day. All the competitors get a T-shirt and all kind of product is given away. The base area turns into a carnival atmosphere with booths and blow up signs and flags touting Mountain Dew. After a very successful run of just over 20 years Shawnee Peak's final race was held in 2016, but plenty of other events will be on the calendar to keep things humming

A SUMMER DAY AT SHAWNEE PEAK

Many skiers believe summer is vacation time at ski areas, and while it's true that employees take whatever time they have in summer months, a typical summer day is anything but lazing about. It was a day in late June when I stopped by to visit with some folks in the office and out on the hill. Obviously, the base lodge was quiet but folks in the office were busy working on plans for the next season and some upcoming summer events.

Mike Harmon transporting a chair for lift maintenance.

Outside I found mountain manager Mike Harmon drivin a tractor near the base of the summit triple chair. Josh Harrington who works inside the office and outside with the ski school in winter was lining up chairs for Harmon to pick up with the tractor. This is part of normal summer maintenance, removing the chair from the cable, inspecting the cable and performing any needed repairs or upgrades on the lift. This team was replacing the chairs.

Once the chair was on the lifting bar of the tractor, Harmon drove to the base of the lift where John Happel sat in the bucket of loader set at the right level for him to access the clamp. As the chair was hoisted into place, Danny Gyger was at the controls of the lift bringing the marked spot on the cable into alignment so Happel could move the clamp into place and tighten it with his wrench.

This process was repeated for each chair until all 162 chairs had been affixed in their new positions on the cable. On the other side of the area, the chairs from the Pines quad were stacked the same way waiting to be reattached to that cable and at the base of the East Chair those chairs were waiting.

Summer is also when lifts get built as this 1969 shot of the Pine Chair construction shows.

Maintaining lifts is an obvious duty but there is a lot more to do at ski areas in summer. The growing season provides plenty of work. If not mowed and brushed out, those ski trails would disappear under a heavy growth and the cost of making the brush disappear under expensive manmade snow would be prohibitive.

We don't see them under the snow while skiing but most trails have water bars to prevent erosion. These are also maintained in summer to keep the surfaces as smooth as possible, again to allow coverage with a minimum amount of snow. The list of summer projects is endless, from base lodge improvements to work on snowmaking pumps, pipes, guns and the base lodge. Obviously, any improvements, new lifts and more are done in summer.

The employees I watched on that day are all on the job in winter, Harmon directing on mountain operations for more than 30 years, Happel overseeing lift operations and Gyger handling the on mountain part of the area's race programs

ED ROCK RETIREMENT

The second Saturday in December, 2016 I visited a ski area without skiing. Shawnee Peak wasn't yet open waiting until the next weekend. But they were getting ready. We could see the snow guns going as we approached the area over the causeway across Moose Pond. They were blowing snow on the Main, the Pines and the upper mountain. A few employees were manning the snowmaking, but most of the rest were in Blizzard's Pub. There we joined them in the room filled with season pass holders and other Shawnee Peak skiers. We were all there to show our appreciation for Ed Rock, who was retiring after 34 years at the helm of Maine's longest continuously operated ski area.

In an emotional presentation Shawnee owner Chet Homer told the gathering how much he appreciated having Ed Rock as GM in the 22 years he has owned the mountain. He cited such events as the ice storm that shut down the area that Ed's leadership in mobilizing employees and outside contractors got the mountain back in operation in days when it easily could have been weeks. "It has been an honor to work with Ed all these years and together we have positioned Shawnee Peak to be a viable long-term ski area," said Homer. "I have been extremely lucky to have had his friendship and guidance. I think many skiers and community members feel the same way."

In recognition of Rock's 34 years of loyal service to the ski area and the community Chet Homer announced the creation of the Ed Rock Community Spirit Fund to benefit the town of Bridgton. Shawnee Peak opened the fund with a $10,000 donation which will be managed by the Maine Community Foundation. An annual payout is being managed by the town of Bridgton, which will determine where the funds will be awarded. Skiers wishing to donate to the fund can do so by going to www.mainecf.org. Click on Give Now and under Designation scroll down to "Ed Rock Community Spirit Fund" and make your contribution.

The reception would not have been complete without hearing from the honoree and Ed Rock stood up to thank everyone present. In every event over the years Ed has avoided the spotlight, always asking others to do the speaking and those of us who know him were not surprised by his remarks. Those arriving at the mountain in the morning would often meet Ed walking through the base lodge, stopping to greet skiers and he seemed to know them all. He asks employees how things are going and encourages them to keep up the good work. This day was no different. He took his time in front of the appreciative crowd to thank the employees who "made his time as manager so enjoyable". He gave credit to employees who showed up to get things going again after the ice storm, noting that many had no power at home but still made their way in to get the mountain back up and running. Ed took the time to name many of the long time employees and some regular skiers for their contributions to skiing at Shawnee Peak.

It was typical Ed Rock, not about himself, but those around him. The new GM, Ralph Lewis grew up in the area and has returned to his roots. Ralph remembered learning to ski at Pleasant Mountain in the seventies when he and the other kids would ride the East T-bar because it was faster than the chair and they could get in more runs. He also remembered how every so often the T-bar would slide up inside the back of the parka of someone unloading and toss them aside. Now he's back with no T-bars and modern chair lifts to oversee. As manager he has a great example to follow. And many days that winter Ed was wandering through the base Lodge as he stayed on as a consultant.

SHAWNEE PEAK AT PLEASANT MOUNTAIN AT 80

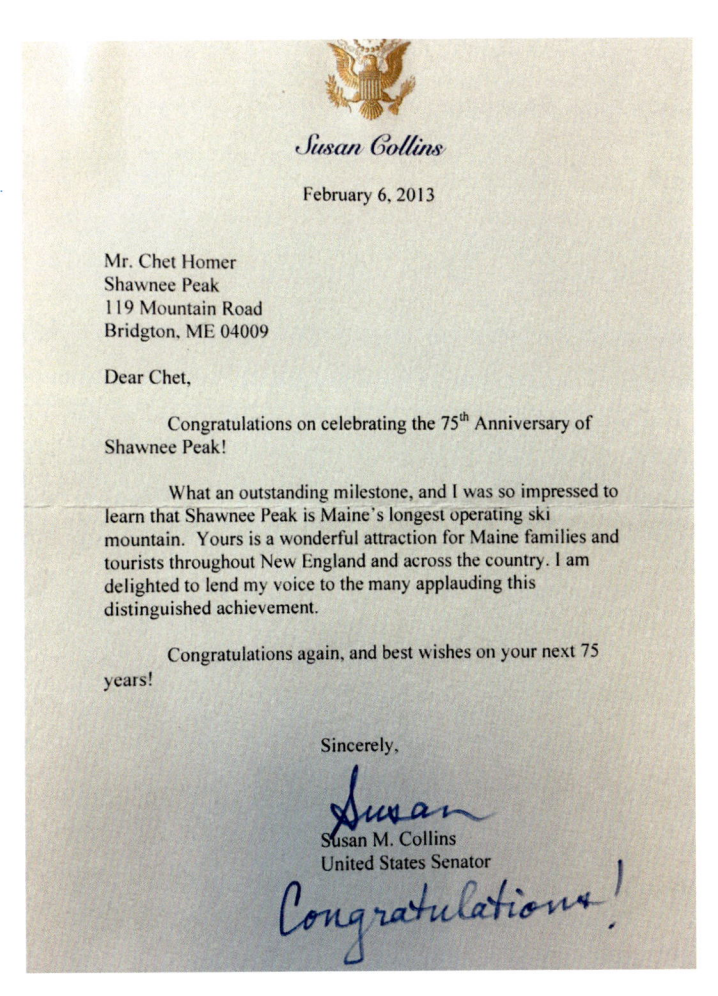

Susan Collins

February 6, 2013

Mr. Chet Homer
Shawnee Peak
119 Mountain Road
Bridgton, ME 04009

Dear Chet,

Congratulations on celebrating the 75th Anniversary of Shawnee Peak!

What an outstanding milestone, and I was so impressed to learn that Shawnee Peak is Maine's longest operating ski mountain. Yours is a wonderful attraction for Maine families and tourists throughout New England and across the country. I am delighted to lend my voice to the many applauding this distinguished achievement.

Congratulations again, and best wishes on your next 75 years!

Sincerely,

Susan M. Collins
United States Senator

Congratulations!

In the 80th season the scene at Shawnee Peak is familiar. On a typical mid week morning a group of regulars can be found changing in the great room. They include a handful of octogenarians, skiers who can remember the very early days of skiing at Pleasant Mountain and they ski every midweek day. For most the day starts early and ends with lunch.

Typical is Bob Fitzimmons. Approaching 90, Bob, a one time patrolman at Pleasant Mountain, was skiing every mid week day. He could be found in a corner of the Great Room every morning booting up with his friends, Jack Farrar of Gorham, Jack Sweetland, Naples, Bob Michaud, County Road, Bridgton, and Paulie Spaulding who vsits the area for six weeks every winter from Ohio. They are often joined by Hans Jenni and his wife Barbara.

Another regular is Clint White of Bridgton who maintains the condos.

One day in March, 2012, the Great Room was occupied, as a room for high school racers who were competing that day. As is often the case that space was set aside for racers and coaches, but Ed Rock had taken care of his regulars. The table where the group usually changes, carried a sign, "Reserved for the Michaud Party".

Another group of regulars who ski daily, draw the envy of many other skiers who watch them carve one perfect turn after another. One can often be seen, carving Royal Christies (A ballet type maneuver similar to a figure skater carving on one skate while extending the other high behind) down the Pines slope. That would be Bruce Cole, who directed the freestyle program during the heyday of the freestyle movement in the seventies. Cole has returned to his home area along with some of the others, Peter Young, Jeff Coffin (Wilie Coyote of the Stump films), and Frank Howell. Another from that era who went on to become one of the top freestyle officials in the world, David Farrar is now a member of the volunteer ski patrol. Another regular midweek skier who draws his share of attention is Billy Dolliver, known to most as "Billy D". Billy skis every midweek day and can usually be seen paired with Cole, Coffin or one of the others all conspicuous by their near perfect technique as they carve turns down the mountain. They don't carry any official titles but retired GM Ed Rock said "It's great to have them out there entertaining our other skiers."

Typical of Shawnee skiers was a pair of friends who started skiing at Pleasant Mountain in the fifties who would drive from the Portland area every Friday evening so they can be on the slopes by the time the lifts open at 8:30 Saturday morning. Like many regulars, Jack Vallely and Mike Keeley would head over to the east area where with a few friends they would make their first runs in the early morning sun. After two or three runs on those trails, it was over to the front side and favorite old runs, Parmalee, Cooley's and the Pine Slope. An easy cruise down Sunset Boulevard was often part of their morning exploration, and before heading in for lunch in Blizzard's Pub, a couple of runs down Jack Spratt to hit the Headwall on the east Slope before skier traffic scraped it down would cap the morning.

This is a Bruce Cole SelfieThree Shawnee veteran regulars, R-L Jeff Coffin, Steve Keith and Bruce Cole. These "Grumpy Old Men" share a chair on the summit triple in 2008 somewhere near mid station.

Mike Keeley told how his mother took them to Pleasant Mountain through the sixties until he reached high school in Falmouth, where other activities crowded out skiing. On graduation he returned to the sport and ski area where he had learned. One of

Fresh snow is always welcome at Shawnee Peak.

the eight owners from the Portland area, Joe Hutchins was building a new place on County Road (The dirt road on the right just before the parking lot when approaching the area from Rte. 302 on Mountain Road) and Keeley was working for him as an electrical contractor. The conversation one day turned to what Hutchins would do with his old place and Mike said, "Why not sell it to me?" He continued, "We wrote out the deal on a napkin in the restaurant and my family skied out of it until we built the East Slope Condos."

His friend Valleley still skied out of a camp on County Road. Although he started at Pleasant Mountain at age five, he wound up skiing at Sugarloaf for 30 years, returning to Pleasant Mountain in 1986. He explained, "A couple of high school buddies skied there so we rented a camp the first year, and bought it the next. We had four families. Two of our three children were in the race program. The kids made me promise never to sell the place at the mountain."

Like his friend Keeley his loyalty to Shawnee Peak went well beyond simply buying a season pass and skiing. When the ski area got a batch of bad diesel fuel at the beginning of one season, Jack had his company, Clean Harbors, on the job within hours and before 24 hours had passed, the tanks had been drained, the fuel cleaned and the compressors ready to go for snowmaking. Ed Rock said, "Whenever we have a problem that calls for his crews's skills, they drop everything and get us going again." Keeley's occupational skills also played a key role at the mountain. After the ice storm in 1998, he and his company worked extensively restoring lights and power lines at the area. Ed Rock, remarked, "When we had an electrical problem on a weekend, having Mike on hand was like having a resident electrician."

Joe Hutchins son Mark was also a member of the group, skiing with them on weekends and for 18 seasons joining them every Thursday evening for Racing with the Moon. Mark's two boys grew up skiing and racing at Shawnee Peak, but both now live in Colorado and do their skiing there.

That group gradually broke up and Keeley admitted that after Vallely's death a few years ago, he no longer got out there every Saturday morning but he is still at the mountain most weekends,

Among Keeley's most enjoyable memories are the evenings spent with his teammates on the Hutchins Trucking team as they piled up victories Racing With the Moon. The team of Keeley, Vallely, Jeff Coffin, Kim Pike, Mark Hutchins, Scott Mc Farland, Steve

Enjoying lunch on the deck.

Hansen and an occasional substitute racked up a dozen season long titles. That was according to Keeley's memory and June Gyger backed him up saying, "It was at least that many".

In the beginning the group raced three nights a week, but over the years it dropped to two and finally one before a combination of age, some knee problems and other demands on time ended the long run of first the Hutchins team and later the T-Buck team.

Racing with the Moon is just one segment of racing at Shawnee Peak. What began at Pleasant Mountain in the early years has simply continued and grown. There are also numerous benefit races, such as the Haggett Memorial Race and the Jack Vallely Memorial Race. There is high school and middle school racing mid week with 100 or more racers at each event, as many as 70 each season. The Shawnee Peak Ski Team operates weekends with sixty plus junior racers from ages 8 to 18, Jan 1st through February. These kids get to travel and race in USSA races and it's typical of programs at many mountains where our

Families can always be found at Shawnee Peak.

future U.S. Ski Team members will come from.

Keeping track of all these programs is a full time job on the mountain and off. For most of the past 30 years June Gyger a former member of the Pleasant Mountain Ski Patrol has handled the coordination of these events. That meant registering racers in the base lodge and moving to the timing building next to the base of the summit triple to time the racers, tasks she handled until her retirement in 2016/17. On the mountain her son Danny Gyger took over the duties from Henry Hudson in 1999 and is still on the job.

As Shawnee Peak at Pleasant Mountain enters its ninth decade skiers are being produced for the future. Whether they ski down the race courses, follow in the ski tracks of the freestylers of the seventies, man the ski schools and ski patrols of the future, or just fill the lifts and slopes like the families have for 80 years, they will keep the slopes busy at Maine's oldest continuously operated ski area.

SKIERS FROM AWAY

One aspect of Shawnee Peak is often overlooked or simply unknown by most skiers. In the seventies and eighties the area was often referred to as the "Commuter Mountain" an assumption that its proximity to Portland made it a day area for those skiers. While that proximity has certainly resulted in a loyal core of skiers from Maine's largest population center, Shawnee and Pleasant Mountain before it has always drawn from more of New England and that is a growing source of skiers.

Chet Homer pointed out, "A great deal of our success now and going forward can be credited to our out of state loyal season pass holders. The majority of kids on the Shawnee Peak Race Team are from out of State and the Hyannis Yacht Club has been here each year for a weekend in January." He went on to note that 75 % of the slope side condo owners are from out of state as are all the guests at the Shawnee Peak House.

Probably because Shawnee Peak doesn't have the thousands of on mountain beds found at the large destination resorts, the perception of a strictly local area is easy to understand. Adding to the perception is a decided lack of hotel rooms in the Bridgton area. Skiers have found the beds they need in some creative ways and one individual has made a significant contribution. Peter Roth started by building a single house on Moose Pond in the late nineties, a house that would sleep 15. Renting to skiers and vacationers in summer filled the house on a regular basis and he built three more creating an important part of Shawnee Peak's bed base. According to Roth, "Skiers come mostly from the South and

Skiers enjoying the sun on the deck.

North Shore and Cape Cod but we get some from as far away as Rhode Island and Connecticut."

Roth pointed out that that there were homes all around the lake that were being rented to skiers in winter and vacationers in summer. By renting homes together families were getting economical vacations. As to why they were choosing Shawnee Peak, "It's the snowmaking and grooming. It's amazing what they do technology." To add to the example of the success of this alternative to hotels Roth noted that in July and August hundreds of skiers were making their plans and reservations for winter.

One season pass holder from Cape Cod who is a leader in bringing more skiers to Shawnee Peak is Jacquie Newson. Since 1989-90 she has been organizing a winter outing for members of the Hyannis Yacht Club. It started with a weekend in January, with fifty people renting the lakeside condos, three families to a condo, in ten units. This has since

"Early skiers from away might have sent this postcard back home.

grown to a three day weekend with over 100 skiers and another fifty or so that look for other forms of recreation.

When asked why Shawnee Peak, Jacquie turned to her husband Roger who started skiing at Pleasant Mountain in the sixties. "We had just started skiing and were looking for someplace inexpensive to build a ski camp. The Bridgton area was just right, land was not as costly as New Hampshire and we had the lakes."

When they were married in 1985 they continued to ski out of the A-Frame on Knight's Hill. She added about the reasons for coming back to Shawnee Peak year after year, "They are the most accommodating people ever, whatever we ask Scott (Scott Condon, head of group sales) for, we get it. We asked to use the air bag for a contest and he said "sure". He roped off part of the deck for a barbecue. The support we get from the staff is always there for us."

Both Newson and Roth mentioned the Shawnee Peak Race Team as important to the skiers from Massachusetts and Cici Gordon, one of the members of the program added the details. "Every Saturday and Sunday we have seventy racers on the hill training for racing in MARA (Maine Alpine Racing Association) events." These are sanctioned races where the kids 8-19 can establish themselves and build official points which are critical if a young racer wants to compete at higher levels. They also try to lure college racers to compete in order to have better points for their races. About 70 percent of the Shawnee kids are from out of state. Gordon said they work to keep it affordable with scholarships and help with equipment.

In Maine programs such as Gould Academy/Sunday River and CVA/Sugarloaf get

As always on a race day skiers gather around the base timing shack to watch for results.

the attention, but programs such as Shawnee Peak provide an affordable route to high level racing without the major expense and occasionally a racer will develop to the point where they will transfer to one of those schools or one of the other ski academies in New England. The team gives young ski racers an opportunity to develop their talents and decide just how far they want to pursue ski racing. For some it will be preparation for ski racing in college. For others this will be the only racing they ever do, but race training always develops better skiers. And, of course, there's always Racing with the Moon.

The skiers mentioned above are only the tip of the iceberg for Shawnee Peak's skiers from away. Peter Roth told how, in addition to renting, a number of skiers from out of state have purchased homes on the lake. Often these summer places had to be winterized, but there was an added benefit. Unlike owning a condo on most mountains, these places have a high rental value in summer. An owner can plan some vacation time for the family, and set aside a few weeks for rentals to defray costs such as taxes. The family part is important as Jacquie Newson remarked, "At Shawnee, we can just let the kids go. We don't have to worry about them." When everything is considered, Shawnee Peak is every bit the ski destination for skiers from away as any place in New England.

THE FUTURE

During Chet Homer's tenure as owner and president of Shawnee Peak skiers have come to expect constant improvement, sometimes small and at other times major, but always an improvement of the experience on the snow and off. At the beginning of the 75th Anniversary season, 2012-2013 I interviewed the owner and asked about the future.

In speculating about the future it's important to know the owner's philosophy about owning a ski area, "I consider myself a steward of the ski area". He went on to explain that his responsibility was to operate Shawnee Peak in a way that would keep it attractive to today's skiers and make it financially viable for skiers yet to come. This explains why there wouldn't be any huge expansion requiring massive debt. The slow steady pace would continue.

While there were a number of desired projects, Homer noted, "We are always looking to enhance the skiing product, especially with snowmaking. We would like to move to 5000-6000 gallons." Those increases would guarantee more and better skiing in the early season while building a deep base for the mid season. His philosophy is simple. "Snowmaking takes precedence over trail expansion."

One change came quickly with an expansion of the beginner area by doubling the length of the magic carpet and the area it serves for that 75th season. Handicapped skiers were given access to the second floor of the base lodge and Blizzard's Pub when special lift was installed on the East end of the lodge. A freestyle airbag was installed and more snowmaking was added.

A Kassbohrer snocat with a power tiller laying out a mat of corduroy.

In the half decade since that interview items have been checked off the wish list. For the 2014-2015 season the beginner double chair was replaced with a triple and the terrain regraded to create a better learning experience for both instructors and new skiers. The almost annual snowmaking up grades included new fan guns and 40 high efficiency HKD guns. The increase in snowmaking capacity has reached just under 4000 gallons with more to be added as needed. To provide better skiing on the area's steepest pitches a winch cat has been added to the fleet.

The next season saw another remodeling of the base lodge adding space on the main floor, a new glade off Moonshot, more high efficiency snowguns, and a new learn to ski program which awarded a free pair of Elan skis after three lessons. That year Shawnee Peak was recognized by the National Ski Areas Association with a Golden Eagle Award for its sustainability programs.

For the 2016-2017 season the rental section in the basement of the base lodge was expanded to speed the process and get skiers on the slopes more quickly, and a new tuning machine was added.

Entering the 80th season most items on the wish list have been accomplished but one is still in the dream stage. That would be more residential units to the West, "I envision a small inn right on the mountain, 10-12 rooms," said Homer.

This would fit in with the desire to add summer activity. With thousands of summer visitors in the area, mostly attracted by the many lakes, there is a high potential to add to the viability of the company as a year round business. The company has property on Rte. 302 and on the mountain to the west which has the potential for both ski area and lodging expansion and options are being studied.

These giant snow guns can turn huge amounts of water into snow.

One thing that is certain about the future is the enthusiasm of Shawnee Peak's owner. While Chet Homer is seen to be a quiet, efficient businessman and considers himself a steward of his ski area, he does admit, "Sometimes while skiing at night, I stand at the top of the mountain and look out over the lighted slopes. That's when I think how lucky I am to own this truly special place." That reveals a devotion not seen by the everyday skier at Shawnee Peak, but it's there and it bodes well for the future as the resort celebrates birthday number 80. As to future ownership, Chet Homer's son Geoff is learning the ropes at Shawnee Peak.

Recognition

Any business that has lasted for 80 years has certainly garnered some recognition, and for a ski area the longevity is even more exceptional. About the time skiing got underway at Pleasant Mountain, there were dozens of rope tows being set up all over New England and plenty right here in Maine. Most are long gone, but Shawnee Peak at Pleasant Mountain thrives. As you have read in these pages, this was the site of the state's first T-bar and a few years later, the first chair lift.

- Over the years the area has received numerous accolades for its innovation, charitable contributions and programs designed to encourage new skiers, especially school children. Here are some of the kudos.
- 1995 10th Mountain Spirit of Skiing Award
- 1998 to present Chet Homer serves on board of New England Ski Areas Council
- 2003 121st Maine Legislature recognized Shawnee Peak on its 65th birthday.
- 2003 Ski Magazine Ski East section ran "Little Gem" story on Shawnee Peak.
- 2005-2011 Chet Homer served on Board of National Ski Areas Association.
- 2005 Shawnee Peak was named among top ten ski areas in North America for "*Best Night Riding*" by Snowboarder Magazine.
- 2007 Received Red Cross Real Hero Award for Outstanding Environmental Service.
- 2008-2017 Chet Homer served as Chairman of NESAC/Snowcountry.
- 2010 Recognized by 157th Air Refueling Wing, Pease ANGD, NH for ongoing support to America's Armed Forces.
- 2011 Boys and Girls Club of Dorchester, MA ski day in January. All expenses including transportation covered by Shawnee Peak for 150 kids, a program that continues to this day.
- 2011 Installed Maine's first lift loading conveyor.
- 2015 Received Ski Magazine's Golden Eagle Award for Environmental Excellence.
- 2017 Established the Ed Rock Community Spirit Award funded by Shawnee Peak at the Maine Community Foundation.

MAINE
SKI HALL OF FAME

Naturally, to make such significant contributions to the sport a ski area has to be populated by leaders and innovators whether in management, competition, instruction, coaching, or volunteering and 14 skiers from Shawnee Peak and Pleasant Mountain have been elected to the Maine Ski Hall of Fame.

Year	Inductee(s)
2003	Russ Haggett, Wes Marco
2004	Greg Stump
2005	James C. Jones Franklyn "FC" Emery
2008	Hans Jenni
2009	Tom Bennett
2011	David Farrar
2012	Frank Howell
2013	Bruce Cole
2014	Tom Gyger
2015	Bruce Chalmers
2016	Geoff Stump
2017	Ed Rock

Photo Credits

Page
1 Ordway pin
1 Early photo
2 Dave Irons photo
3 Brochure from BHS *
4 Patch Photo from Bruce Cole
5 Erickson *
6 Erickson *
6 Erickson *
6 Photo from BHS*
7 Dave Irons Photo
8 Brochure from BHS*
9 Jenni Photo
9 Ray Erickson   Henry Hudson Studio
10 Bruce Cole Photo
10 Shawnee Peak Photo
11 Jenni Photo
12 Jenni Photo
13 BrucCole Photo
14 Jenni ads
14 Patch
15 Bruce Cole Photo
16 Erickson *
17 Groomer Photos Shawnee collection
18 Bruce Cole Photo
19 Patch
19 Bruce Cole Photo
20 Donuts Bruce Cole Photo
20 Pin
22 Pleasant Mt Ad
23 Dining room
23 Dining Room after fire
25 Lights Shawnee Peak Photo
26 Shawnee Peak Photo
28 Bruce cole pic
29 Pin
29 Shawnee Peak Photo
30 Shawnee Peak Photo
31 Shawnee Peak Photo
32 Shawnee Peak Photo
33 Shawnee Peak Photo
34 Shawnee Peak Photos
35 Shawnee Peak Photo
36 Shawnee Peak Photo
37 Shawnee Peak Photo
38 Bruce Cole Photo
39 Shawnee Peak Photo
40 Shawnee Peak Photo
40 Shawnee Peak Photo
43 Bruce Cole Photo
44 Shawnee Peak Photo
45 Shawnee Peak Photo
46 Shawnee Peak Photo
47 Dave Irons Photo
48 Old Post Card
49 Dave Irons Photo
50 Shawnee Peak Photo
51 Shawnee Peak Photo

* Ray Erickson's family donated an album of his pictures and these are from that album.
* BHS = Bridgton Historical Society

Made in the USA
Lexington, KY
15 November 2017